WHY YOU ARE UNHAPPY

THE REAL REASONS YOU FEEL EMPTY AND HOW TO STOP LYING TO YOURSELF

HARRY PAGANCOSS

TABLE OF CONTENTS

INTRODUCTION

This little book won't fix you, and it's not trying to. But if you're reading it, you're either unhappy—or wise enough to sense you're drifting in that direction.

Deep down, many people don't feel happy. Traumas we cling to, definitions inherited from others, and emotional baggage we collect along the way wrap around us like a suffocating blanket.

If you're feeling unhappy, remember: you still have the power to shift your inner climate.

And if happiness feels out of reach, take this moment as a sign that something in you is waking up—ready to do something different.

You know life isn't perfect, but you've chased relief like your sanity depended on it. Prayers, meditations, vision boards—anything that promised peace. Maybe they helped, but only long enough to numb the ache and push it further down the road. They soothe, but they don't solve. They distract, but they don't free you. I know this too well.

At some point, the medicine stops curing and only dulls the symptoms. That's when you stop chasing comfort and start facing the truth. That's where this book begins.

You might feel stuck. And stuck feels a lot like unhappy.

It feels like something's off. Like the life you're living doesn't match the life you're built for. Like happiness should be here by now, and somehow, it isn't.

Here's the truth: you're not unhappy because you're failing. You're unhappy because you're human.

And being human means carrying contradictions, repeating patterns, mistaking fear for safety, and performance for connection.

It means doing the things that hurt you and calling them love, loyalty, and responsibility.

This book won't guide you, but it will reflect you.

It won't tell you what to do, but it will show you what you're already doing, and why it costs so much of your peace.

Some of it will sting. That's how you know it's real.

Awareness is the first step to freedom. You can't change what you can't see.

So let's look.

PART ONE

THE PERFORMANCE

WHY YOU'RE TIRED OF PUTTING ON AN ACT

YOU MISTAKE
RIGHTEOUSNESS FOR PEACE

You believe you're standing up for the truth. But in reality, you're only defending your desire to be right.

There's a specific kind of high that comes from correcting someone. From diagnosing their soul. From knowing—*really knowing*—that you've got it figured out and they don't.

You are so sure.

It feels like clarity. Like conviction. But it's not peace.

Peace doesn't need to win arguments. It doesn't need to save strangers in parking lots or salon chairs. It doesn't clench its teeth while saying, "Have a blessed day."

Righteousness is loud. It interrupts. It assigns meaning to other people's lives without asking.

Peace is quiet. It listens and cherishes. It allows people to be wrong without needing to fix them. You're unhappy because you've confused this with righteousness. And the truth is, righteousness is easier. It gives you a role, a mission, and an enemy. Peace simply gives you peace, and that can terrify you.

Peace doesn't need an audience or validation.

It begins when you let go of the need to always be right and pretending to have all the answers.

YOU'RE EXHAUSTED FROM PRETENDING

You smile when you're sad. You say "I'm fine" when you're falling apart. You laugh at jokes that aren't funny and agree with opinions you don't hold. Because it's easier than being honest, and you'd rather agree and be liked.

But pretending takes energy; you're running out of steam, functioning on fumes.

You've spent so long performing that you've forgotten what it feels like just to *be*.

To say what you mean. To feel what you feel. To stop managing everyone else's comfort at the expense of your own.

And now you're so far from yourself, you don't even know how to get back.

You're unhappy because you've been playing a role for so

long that you've forgotten you're allowed to quit and start again.

You don't owe anyone a performance, not even you.

The people who matter will love you more for the truth than the act.

YOU'RE TERRIFIED
OF BEING SEEN

You want love, but you fear being truly known.

You fear knowing yourself just as much.

So you present the version of you that's easiest to accept—
not the truest one.

The polished one. The manageable one.

The one that never asks for too much, or needs too deeply.
And you convince yourself that's enough.

But it isn't because it's not real. And you know it.

You feel the crack every time you pretend you don't. Even
when people say they love you, you don't believe them.
How could you?

They're loving the mask, not the person beneath it.

And you're exhausted from holding it in place.

Yet the alternative—letting someone see you—feels like handing them a weapon.

What if they leave? What if they judge you? What if the real you is not enough?

So you stay hidden. Safe. Lonely. Unseen.

You're unhappy because you reject yourself first, before anyone else has the chance.

No one can love the real you if you keep hiding yourself.

Allowing yourself to be seen is the price of being known.

And eventually, hiding becomes more painful than the risk of being open.

YOU CONFUSE INTENSITY FOR CONNECTION

You think the relationships that hurt the most are the ones that matter the most.

The ones that keep you up at night and where you feel compelled to prove yourself constantly. Relationships like these feel like emotional whiplash and require constant and intense work.

You call it passion. Depth. Real love.

But it's not. It's just chaos with a pulse.

Real connection doesn't drain you. It requires no shrinking, performing, or guessing. It actually feels good.

It's steady. It's safe. It's boring in the best way.

But you don't trust that. Because somewhere along the way, you learned that love is supposed to hurt. That if it's easy, it's not real.

So you chase the highs. The drama. The people who make you feel alive by making you feel like you're dying.

And you call the calm ones "nice" and move on.

You're unhappy because you've mistaken turbulence for depth.

And the truth is, you're exhausted. You don't know how to stop. You're addicted.

Love isn't meant to be a survival instinct.

A genuine connection feels like a deep breath of satisfaction—a warm, embracing feeling.

5

PERFECTIONISM IS JUST
FEAR WITH A TO-DO LIST

You tell yourself you have high standards.

But really, you're just terrified of being judged.

So you don't start the project until you know it'll be perfect. You don't share the work until it's flawless. You don't try the thing unless you're sure you'll succeed.

And you call it excellence.

But it's not. It's paralysis.

Because perfect doesn't exist. And while you're waiting for it, life is passing you by.

You're not creating. You're not growing. You're not risking. You're just... stuck. You've even perfected the art of being stuck.

Polishing something that will never be done. Protecting yourself from failure by never trying.

And calling it discipline, the right time, precision.

But perfectionism isn't about doing it right. It's about avoiding being wrong.

You're unhappy because you've built a prison out of impossible standards and called it ambition.

Done is better than perfect. And perfect is just another word for afraid.

You are already perfect; what you do has nothing to do with it.

6

PRIDE BECAME YOUR IMAGE, NOT YOUR TRUTH

You don't take pride in who you are. You take pride in who people *think* you are.

The carefully curated version. The highlight reel. The carefully filtered life you post and perform. The perfect angle.

You measure worth in likes. In comments. In how many people saw you winning.

But inside, you're exhausted. You feel like an impostor.

Because the image takes work. And the truth? The truth is messy. Unglamorous. Unpostable. Insecure.

So you hide it.

You double down on the performance. You chase validation as if it were oxygen.

And you call it confidence.

But it's not. It's just fear dressed up in good lighting.

Real pride is quiet. It doesn't need an audience. It is unassumingly confident and elegant.

You're unhappy because you've built a life that appears successful but feels empty. You do not live it for yourself, but for others.

And no amount of applause will fill that.

You can't find peace by forcing your way into it.

At some point, you have to stop pretending and start embracing the true feeling of peace within.

PART TWO
THE TRAP

WHY YOU'RE STUCK IN
PATTERNS YOU CAN'T SEE

YOU'RE ADDICTED TO
YOUR OWN SUFFERING

You say you want to be happy. But every time you get close, you sabotage it.

You pick fights. You catastrophize. You dig up old wounds and examine them like artifacts. You open old wounds as if they were presents.

Because suffering is familiar. And happiness? Happiness is vulnerable.

When you're suffering, you have a story. You have a reason. You're the underdog, the survivor, the one who's been through it. You are the victim.

When you're happy, you're just... happy. And that's terrifying. Because what if it doesn't last? What if you lose it?

So you don't let yourself have it in the first place.

You stay in the relationship that drains you. You keep the job that crushes you. You replay the argument in your head for the hundredth time.

Not because you have to. Because it's safer than admitting you could walk away.

Suffering gives you control. Happiness asks you to let go. And you're not ready for that.

Stop feeding the wound and calling it depth.

Stop polishing old scars as if they're proof of a life well-lived. That's how you stay trapped.

Healing doesn't erase your story—it rewrites the ending.

YOU THINK PEACE
MEANS GIVING UP

You've been taught that if you're not stressed, you're not trying hard enough.

That rest is laziness. That boundaries are selfish. That if you're not grinding, you're falling behind.

So you wear exhaustion like a badge. You brag about how little you slept—three hours, maybe four. How busy you are. How much is on your plate.

And when someone suggests you slow down, you hear: *Give up. Be mediocre. Stop caring.*

You get defensive, even insulted.

The truth is that peace isn't about surrendering. It's a strategy.

It's knowing that you can't pour from an empty cup. That burnout isn't a rite of passage, and that you're allowed to exist without justifying your worth through productivity.

You're unhappy because you think happiness is the reward for suffering long enough.

But it's not. Happiness is what happens when you stop treating your life like a war you have to win.

Peace isn't retreating and giving up.

It's about choosing your energy as if it's worth something.

9
YOU THINK YOU CAN CONTROL WHAT YOU CAN'T

You plan. You prepare. You try to predict every outcome.

And when life doesn't cooperate, you panic.

Because you've built your sense of safety on the illusion of control.

Most of life is out of your hands; that is the truth.

You can't control other people. You can't control the economy. You can't control whether someone loves you back, or the calls at work, or whether the test comes back clean.

You can only control your response.

But that feels too small. Too powerless.

So you keep trying to manage the unmanageable. You overthink. You overplan. You exhaust yourself trying to eliminate risk.

And you call it responsibility.

But it's not. It's fear disguised as readiness.

You're unhappy because you're white-knuckling your way through life, trying to control things that were never yours to manage.

And the tighter you grip, the more it slips away.

Let go or be dragged.

Peace starts when you stop trying to control everything and start trusting yourself to handle anything.

YOU'RE LOYAL TO
THE WRONG THINGS

You stay in the job that's killing you because you've been there five years.

You keep the friend who drains you because you've known them since high school.

You hold onto the version of yourself you were a decade ago because letting go feels like failure.

But loyalty isn't supposed to hurt.

It's not supposed to cost you your peace, your health, your joy.

And yet you wear it like armor. You call it integrity. Commitment. Being a good person.

But really, it's just fear.

Fear of change. Fear of being judged. Fear of admitting that what once worked no longer does.

You're unhappy because you're still honoring contracts you never signed.

And the truth is, you're allowed to evolve, to change your mind. You're allowed to outgrow things. People. Versions of yourself.

Loyalty to your own well-being isn't betrayal. It's the most basic type of survival.

Loyalty isn't a virtue when it costs you your peace.

Leave before you disappear.

YOU'RE WAITING
FOR PERMISSION

You're waiting for someone to tell you it's okay.

To rest. To say no. To walk away. To want something different. To be happy.

But no one's coming.

Because the people around you benefit from your guilt. From your people-pleasing. From your belief that your needs come last.

So you stay stuck. Waiting for the perfect moment. The right sign. Someone else to go first.

But permission doesn't arrive. You have to take it.

And that feels selfish. Reckless. Wrong.

Because you've been taught that good people sacrifice, that love means staying. That loyalty means suffering in silence.

The truth is that you're allowed to choose yourself.

Not because you've earned it. Not because everyone agrees. Because you're alive, and your life belongs to you.

You're unhappy because you're still waiting for someone to hand you the keys to your own cage.

They won't. You already have them and wear them as a pendant around your neck.

No one can free you from a cage you keep locked from the inside.

YOU'RE COMPARING YOUR INSIDES TO EVERYONE ELSE'S OUTSIDES

You see their vacation photos. Their promotions. Their perfect relationships.

And you feel like you're falling behind.

But here's what you're actually comparing: Your messy, unfiltered reality to their carefully curated highlight reel.

You're measuring your worth against a performance, and losing.

Because they're not showing you the fights. The debt. The anxiety. Most likely, they also feel like they're failing at times. But you won't see that.

They're showing you the win. The angle. The filter.

And you're taking it as evidence that you're not enough.

But comparison isn't insight. It's theft.

It steals your peace. Your progress. Your ability to see your own life clearly.

You're unhappy because you're using someone else's edited version as the standard for your unedited truth.

And that's a game you'll never win.

You're not late.

You're living a different story, at a different pace.

Stop using someone else's script to judge your own life.

Don't be an extra in someone else's play.

Be your story, not the end of it.

PART THREE

THE ERASURE

WHY YOU'VE DISAPPEARED
FROM YOUR OWN LIFE

13
YOU STOPPED SHOWING UP FOR YOURSELF

You call it humility. But really, it's just self-abandonment.

You don't even wear your favorite clothes or cologne anymore—you're saving them for a life you're not living.

You put everyone else first. You say yes when you mean no. You skip meals, cancel plans with yourself, and ignore your own needs because someone else's always feel more urgent.

And you think that makes you good.

But it doesn't. It makes you invisible.

Even to yourself.

You've stopped checking in and stopped asking what *you* need. Stopped treating your own life like it matters.

And now you resent everyone you've been bending for.

Not because they asked too much. But because you never asked for anything at all.

They weren't ungrateful — they never asked for all you gave, but you offered it anyway at a cost to yourself.

Self-respect isn't selfish. It's the foundation of being ourselves.

And you can't build a life on ground you refuse to stand on.

You can't pour from a cup you never fill.

And calling that sacrifice doesn't make it noble—it makes it slow erasure.

YOU CONFUSE EMPATHY WITH ERASURE

You feel everything. Everyone's pain. Everyone's stress. Everyone's mood.

And you think that makes you kind; you celebrate and glorify your sensitivity.

But somewhere along the way, empathy became absorption. You stopped feeling *with* people and started feeling *for* them.

You take on their emotions as if they were yours to carry. You fix. You soothe. You manage everyone's feelings but your own.

And when you finally collapse, you wonder why no one notices.

Because you taught them not to.

You made yourself the emotional infrastructure—the one who holds it all together. And now you're crumbling, and they don't even see the cracks. They've moved on and overcome their pain. But you now carry it.

Empathy without boundaries isn't love. It's self-destruction with good intentions.

You're unhappy because you've confused care with disappearing.

And the truth is, you can hold space for someone without losing yourself in it.

Compassion doesn't require you to drown.

You're allowed to throw the life raft without jumping in.

That's the difference.

YOU THINK VULNERABILITY IS WEAKNESS

You've built walls so high that you can't see over them.

You don't ask for help. You don't admit when you're struggling. You handle everything alone because that's what strong people do.

But you're not strong. You're just isolated.

And you're exhausted from carrying everything by yourself.

However, asking for help often feels like a sign of weakness or failure. Like admitting you're not enough.

So you don't.

You smile and say, "I'm fine." You decline offers of support. You push people away before they get too close.

And then you wonder why you feel so alone.

You're unhappy because you think vulnerability is a sign of weakness.

But it's not. It's actually the only way to connect.

And connection is the only thing that makes any of this bearable.

Let someone see you before you collapse from invisibility.

That's what strength actually looks like.

16

YOU MISTAKE BUSYNESS
FOR PURPOSE

Your calendar is packed. Your to-do list is endless.

And you wear it like proof that you matter.

But busyness is not purpose. It's when purpose stops being your passion.

You're running from meeting to meeting, task to task, never stopping long enough to ask: *Why am I doing this?*

You forgot why.

Because if you stopped, you'd have to face the possibility that none of it means anything.

That you're busy for the sake of being busy. That you've confused motion with direction.

And that can be terrifying.

You keep moving forward, saying yes to everything and filling your days with distractions, leaving no space for doubt or reflection. You look present, but you're living in the future.

However, exhaustion isn't achievement.

And at the end of the day, when you collapse into bed, you don't feel fulfilled. You feel tired.

You're unhappy because you've been sprinting on a treadmill, mistaking speed for progress.

Slow down long enough to remember where you're actually trying to go.

Purpose isn't loud. It's clear and it's pure joy.

17
YOU SCROLL INSTEAD OF WONDER

You're bored. So you reach for your phone.

You're not bored, but you find reasons to pick up your phone and reconnect. "I remembered I need to search for this," "Let me check if I received that email," or "Let me see the new posts."

Honestly, it's not about seeking something; it's about avoiding the discomfort of feeling aimless, idle, and alone with your thoughts. You're afraid of being left alone with yourself.

You scroll. You swipe. You consume. Other people's lives. Other people's thoughts. Other people's curated joy.

And you call it a connection.

But it's not. It's numbing.

You've replaced curiosity with consumption. Wonder with distraction.

You don't ask questions anymore. You don't sit in silence. You don't let your mind wander into the strange, uncomfortable, beautiful places it used to go.

You... scroll.

And wonder why nothing feels new.

You're unhappy because you've traded aliveness for availability.

And the cost is higher than you think.

Curiosity is the antidote to emptiness.

But you have to put the phone down long enough to feel it.

PART FOUR
THE ILUSSION
WHY YOU'RE CHASING THE WRONG THING

18
YOU THINK HAPPINESS IS SUPPOSED TO FEEL LIKE SOMETHING ELSE

You're waiting for happiness to arrive like a package. With confetti. A soundtrack. Perhaps a montage or a vision board.

But happiness, for the most part, doesn't announce itself. Sometimes it's loud; other times, it's subtle. It doesn't walk into your room to draw your attention.

You've been conditioned to expect *stimulation*— notifications, drama, dopamine hits, problems to solve, fires to put out.

So when things are calm, you panic. You think something's wrong. You go looking for trouble because silence feels like emptiness.

Actually, happiness isn't a sudden rush. It isn't a fleeting high. Instead, it's the lack of needing that rush in the first place.

It's boring. It's steady. It doesn't photograph well. Moments are enjoyable and rewarding. Happiness is a mindset that lasts long-term if you nurture it.

And because you've spent years chasing the feeling of *almost happy*—the chase, the fix, the next thing—you've forgotten what actual contentment feels like.

It feels like nothing. And that's precisely why you keep missing it.

Maybe happiness has been here all along —you just kept looking for fireworks instead of quiet soul-level peace and light.

19

YOU'RE AFRAID OF
BEING ORDINARY

You think if you're not exceptional, you're invisible.

So you chase achievement. Recognition. Proof that you matter.

You measure your worth in accomplishments. In likes. In how busy you are. In how much you've overcome.

And it's never enough. Because the bar keeps moving, and you keep moving with it.

The reality is: You don't have to be extraordinary to deserve peace.

You don't have to earn rest, or joy, or love.

You're allowed to be ordinary. To have a quiet life. To not stand out.

Ordinary isn't a flaw; it's a human setting. It is relative.

It only feels like a downgrade because you swallowed someone else's definition of what a "worthy" life looks like.

Ordinary is just a word; you give it meaning. You provide it with shame.

You're unhappy because you think happiness is a reward for being special.

But it's not. It's what happens when you stop trying to outrun yourself.

You don't have to be extraordinary to matter.

You just have to be real enough to stay— and honest enough to question the beliefs that keep telling you you're not enough.

20

YOU THINK YOU'RE SUPPOSED
TO HAVE IT ALL FIGURED OUT

You're in your 30s. 40s. 50s. And you still don't know what you're doing.

You thought you'd have answers by now. A plan. A clear sense of purpose.

But instead, you're winging it. Pretending. Googling "how to be confident" and closing the tab halfway through because even the internet can't fix this.

And you feel like a fraud.

Because everyone else seems so sure, so put together. So confident.

They're not.

They are better at pretending.

The truth is that no one has it figured out. Not really. We're all just making decisions with incomplete information and hoping for the best.

But you're unhappy because you think you're the only one who's lost.

You're not. You're just human.

And maybe the point isn't to figure it all out. Perhaps it's to stop pretending you're supposed to.

You don't need a map when the road is made by walking.

21

YOU'RE ADDICTED
TO NOSTALGIA

You keep looking back.

At the job you used to have. The person you used to be. The time when things felt easier.

And you've convinced yourself that *then* was better than *now*.

But it wasn't. There is a reason you moved on. Intended or not, things had to change.

You're just editing the past with the gift of distance. You're remembering the highlights and forgetting the hard parts.

And using it as proof that you've lost something.

But you haven't. You've just changed.

And change feels like loss when you're not ready to let go.

So you romanticize the past. You replay it. You live in it.

And you miss the present entirely.

You're not happy because you're trying to live in a memory instead of building a life.

Nostalgia is a beautiful place to visit. But you can't live there.

The life you're looking for is happening right now.

22

YOU THINK HAPPINESS
IS SOMETHING YOU FIND

You're searching for it, constantly and religiously.

In the next job. The next relationship. The next city. The next version of yourself.

In the new meditation app. The next book. The next party or vacation trip.

You think happiness is out there somewhere, waiting for you to arrive, to show you the plug so you can hook yourself to it.

But it's not.

Happiness isn't a tangible thing or a physical destination. It's not a reward you earn or a mental state you reach. Instead, it's a way of practicing.

It's the small choices you make every day. The boundaries you set. The gratitude you notice. The peace you protect.

It's not something you find. It's something you build.

And you've been so busy looking for it elsewhere that you missed it growing quietly in the life you already have.

You're unhappy because you keep waiting for happiness to happen *to* you.

But it won't. You have to choose it—every single day. You are you, and that is enough to get it, taste it, feel it, hear it in the now.

Stop searching. Start building.

Happiness isn't hiding.

It's just waiting for you to notice it and give it the attention you give to everyone and everything else but you.

Happiness is already here.

EPILOGUE

You made it.

And that matters more than you think.

Because most people won't even pick up a book like this, they'll keep scrolling. Keep pretending. Keep waiting for happiness to find them.

But you didn't. I commend you for it.

It took me a moment to reflect on why I had been unhappy in the past, and share it here. There are many more reasons we use as crutches for our unhappiness; I thought 22 would suffice.

So, you looked. You sat with the uncomfortable truths. You recognized yourself in these pages—maybe more than you wanted to.

And that takes courage and awareness.

Not the loud, showy type. The subtle kind. The one that indicates I'm ready to face myself honestly, even if it stings.

So here's what I want you to know:

You're not unhappy because you're doing life wrong, but because you're doing it like everyone else told you to.

And now you get to choose differently.

Not all at once. Not perfectly. Just one honest choice at a time — the kind that brings you back to yourself.

Maybe it's setting a boundary you've been avoiding. Perhaps it's letting go of the loyalty that's killing you. Maybe it's admitting you don't have it all figured out—and that's okay.

Maybe it's just putting the phone down and sitting with yourself for five minutes without needing to fix, perform, or prove anything.

That's where it starts.

Not in some grand transformation. But in the quiet decision to stop abandoning yourself. To show up for yourself, wear the nice shirt you love, not just on special occasions, but because you love how it feels.

Don't just be a spectator in others' lives; instead, take charge as the director, actor, and producer of your own. Do it for yourself, not for others.

Unhappiness is something you choose to find.

Happiness is something you build.

One boundary at a time. One present moment at a time. One choice to stop pretending and start being.

And you've already started.

By reading this. By recognizing yourself. By being willing to look.

That's the most challenging part.

Now comes the practice.

I won't sugarcoat it—living this way won't always be straightforward. Occasionally, you'll fall into old habits, like people-pleasing or scrolling aimlessly instead of feeling your emotions. You might find yourself seeking validation or desperately holding onto control.

There will be moments when you retreat and focus on your shortcomings. Sometimes, it will feel as if everything is against you, and no matter how much effort you put in, happiness will seem out of reach. These feelings are part of being here.

That's okay. You're human.

But now you'll notice. And noticing changes everything.

Because once you see the cage, you can't unsee it. And once you see the keys, you can't pretend they're not in your hand.

So here's my hope for you:

That you stop waiting for permission. That you stop performing peace and start protecting it. That you let yourself be ordinary, messy, and real—and discover that's precisely where happiness lives.

Not in the highlight reel. Not in the next achievement. Not in being extraordinary.

But in the simple, quiet, unfiltered truth of who you are when no one's watching.

That's where you'll find it. Not out there. Right here.

You've always had it. You just forgot to look.

Welcome back—time to be happy.

The End.

ABOUT HARRY

Harry Pagancoss is a transformation specialist, author, and former media host with more than two decades of experience helping people turn life's transitions into turning points. He's built businesses, lost them, rebuilt himself, and learned that the work that matters isn't about achievement—it's about becoming whole. He now lives in the countryside outside Atlanta, where he believes happiness isn't something you find; it's something you build.

This is Harry's third book.